CHARITIES IN ACTION

PROTECTING AND CARING FOR CHILDREN

Louise Spilsbury

www.raintreepublishers.co.uk
Visit our website to find out
more information about
Raintree books.

To order:
☎ Phone 0845 6044371
🖷 Fax +44 (0) 1865 312263
🖳 Email myorders@raintreepublishers.co.uk

Customers from outside the UK please telephone +44 1865 312262

Raintree is an imprint of Capstone Global Library
Limited, a company incorporated in England and
Wales having its registered office at 7 Pilgrim Street,
London, EC4V 6LB – Registered company number:
6695582

Text © Capstone Global Library Limited 2012
First published in hardback in 2012
The moral rights of the proprietor have been
asserted.

Edited by Andrew Farrow, Adam Miller, and
  Diyan Leake
Designed by Victoria Allen
Picture research by Ruth Blair
Illustrations by Oxford Designers & Illustrators
Originated by Capstone Global Library Ltd
Printed and bound in China by Leo Paper
  Products Ltd

ISBN 978 1 406 23847 1 (hardback)
16 15 14 13 12
10 9 8 7 6 5 4 3 2 1

British Library Cataloguing in Publication Data
Spilsbury, Louise.
Protecting and caring for children. -- (Charities in
action)
362.7'1-dc23
A full catalogue record for this book is available from
the British Library.

Acknowledgements
The author and publisher are grateful to the following
for permission to reproduce copyright material:
Alamy pp. 21 (© Charles O. Cecil), 35 (© Eddie Gerald),
40 (© Richard G. Bingham II), 49 (© First Light); Photo
provided courtesy of Big Brothers Big Sisters p. 15);
Corbis pp. 5 (© Joel Stettenheim), 11 (© Phillipe
Lissac/Godong), 12 (© Paul Hackett/In Pictures), 23
(© William Campbell), 25 (© Andrew Aitchison/In
Pictures), 28 (© Anthony Asael/Art in All of Us), 32
(© Ralf-Finn Hestoft), 36 (© Eleanor Bentall), 47 (© Bill
Gentile); Getty Images pp. 9 (Luis Ascui/Save The
Children), 17 (David Gillanders), 18 (Bruno Morandi),
26 (Thony Belizaire/AFP), 39 (Per-Anders Pettersson),
43 (Oleg Nikishin/Newsmakers), 45 (Spencer Platt),
53 (Tiziana Fabi/AFP); Shutterstock pp. 13 (© Brad
Thompson), 14 (© Helga Esteb), 51 (© africa924), 55
(© spfotocz), 57 (© Poznyakov).

Cover photograph of an aid worker and child in
Namibia reproduced with permission of Alamy
(© Ace Stock Limited).

CONTENTS

Words printed in **bold** are explained in the glossary.

HELPING CHILDREN

Max's story

Max ran away from home on a Saturday night, because his dad was drunk and had been violently hitting and kicking him again. Max was cold, bruised, scared, and had nowhere to go. Luckily, he had a phone with him and he called a helpline. The **counsellor** he spoke to asked a **volunteer** to pick him up and take him to a safe place until he could be found somewhere to live and a new school. Max says, "As soon as I met my charity worker I felt that at last someone was looking out for me. She helped me get through it all and now I'm getting on with my life."

Workers for many different charities around the world help children like Max experience safer, more enriching lives. Children today face many different kinds of problems, from **abuse** and neglect to a lack of access to a school or hospital. This is why there are different kinds of children's charities. Some children's charities focus on one specific issue, such as helping children who live on the streets; others work with children in one particular region, helping them to tackle any type of problem. There are large charities that have offices and workers across the world, such as Save the Children, and smaller charities located in, say, a single city. They all work to protect and care for vulnerable young people.

How charities work

A charity is an organization that is set up to help people or animals. Most children's charities work to help children in direct ways, such as by providing medicine or shelter, and by running **campaigns** to influence governments to make laws to help to protect children. Charities are independent organizations, so they are not a part of a government department or local authority. They have to raise funds to pay for the help that they provide and the staff they employ. Any profits they make are used to continue their charitable work.

Raising funds for Barnardo's

Nicola Helme is a student programme officer for the UK children's charity Barnardo's. She helps student volunteers organize fundraising events on behalf of the charity:

In my role, I have a lot of freedom to use my initiative to develop activities which benefit students and support the vital work that Barnardo's Children's Services do. Being a part of such a beneficial organization is very satisfying – I am proud to work for Barnardo's. I also enjoy working with the student volunteers as they are so passionate about what they do – there is always a positive atmosphere at their events.

Developing new fundraising initiatives is the most challenging aspect of my role as charity fundraising is very competitive, particularly when money is tight and funding for charities is being reduced. However, it enables me to be creative, develop ideas, and hopefully see them through to delivery of successful, profitable events.

Many people want to help others in need. Some give direct, like this man giving cash to a homeless family in New York. Others give to charities that dispense the aid.

How charities raise funds

Workers and volunteers for children's charities use a variety of ways to raise people's awareness of their cause and to collect money. They organize street fundraising in which teams of workers sign up passers-by to give money by direct debit or standing order. They send out letters, knock on doors, and set up challenge events, such as marathons or mountain climbs, through which the individuals taking part raise money. Some charities sell new and donated goods through shops, mail-order catalogues, and online stores. Charities also place advertisements in newspapers, on radio, on TV, and online to persuade people to donate to their cause.

The cost of fundraising

Supporters want as much of the money they give to charity to go to the people who really need it, but fundraising costs money, too. Most charities say that, overall, it costs between 15p and 25p to raise £1. This sounds a lot, but it costs money to work with existing supporters and to recruit new supporters, and it is vital work.

Who works for children's charities?

Volunteers are very important to the majority of children's charities. Without them, some fundraising efforts, such as shops and community events, would not make any money.

Charities also need to employ people to do skilled jobs and to recruit, manage, and train the volunteers. Big charities employ many people!

- Fund managers come up with ideas for new campaigns.
- Press officers suggest news stories to TV, radio, and other **media** reporters to get stories about children's issues or fundraising needs into the news, and they may give interviews, too.
- Project workers help children in particular projects, such as providing schools with books.
- Other workers fill out applications for grants, design advertising

campaigns for TV and other media, and buy advertising space in papers to bring in new supporters. Some write and send out mailings to the public, and **web designers** create and manage fundraising databases.

The debate over private companies

Some people object to charities paying private companies to do some of their work – for example, paying a company to run a website that collects donations online. Others point out that it is worth paying private companies to do certain jobs because they increase charity funds.

In this book you'll find out about how workers and volunteers for children's charities help young people around the world.

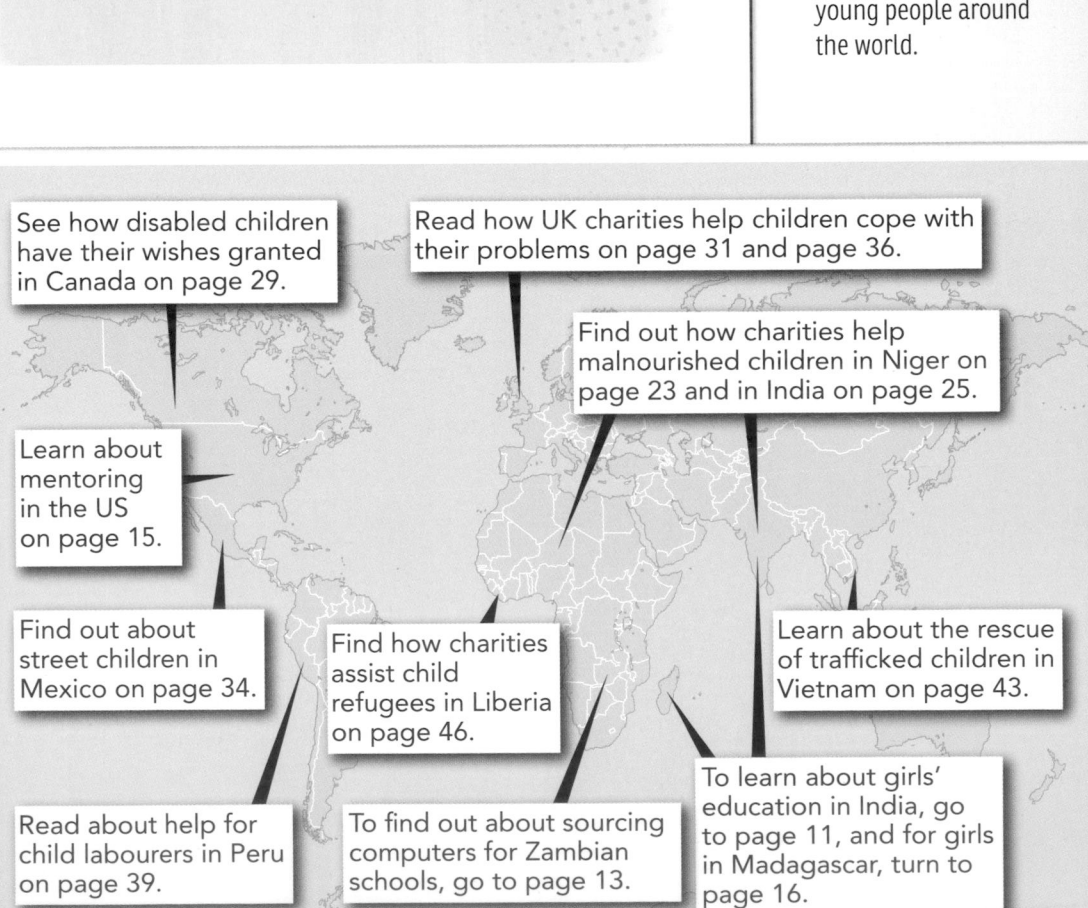

See how disabled children have their wishes granted in Canada on page 29.

Read how UK charities help children cope with their problems on page 31 and page 36.

Find out how charities help malnourished children in Niger on page 23 and in India on page 25.

Learn about mentoring in the US on page 15.

Find out about street children in Mexico on page 34.

Find how charities assist child refugees in Liberia on page 46.

Learn about the rescue of trafficked children in Vietnam on page 43.

Read about help for child labourers in Peru on page 39.

To find out about sourcing computers for Zambian schools, go to page 13.

To learn about girls' education in India, go to page 11, and for girls in Madagascar, turn to page 16.

EDUCATION AND OPPORTUNITIES

Every child has the **right** to an education. Yet today there are 93 million primary-school-age children out of school. Worldwide, only 60 per cent of older children attend secondary school.

Access to schools

The main reason children miss out on school is poverty. Globally, nearly 250 million children miss school to work to help their families; other families cannot afford to pay for uniforms or school books even if schooling is free. Without an education, these children are less likely to be able to get a job in the future.

Mahder's story

Mahder is a boy who lives in Ethiopia, where many families cannot afford to send their children to school:

"I'm 12 and I love running, playing volleyball and watching Ethiopian Pop Idol. My dad was a tailor. He died a few years ago. When he was alive I went to school and always had enough to eat. I was so sad when he died. I went to school for a month and then the money ran out and I had to stop going. When my friends went to school, I would cry all day. I didn't do much apart from look at old school books and help mum ... It makes me angry that not all children in Ethiopia get the chance to go to school."

Primary school age children out of school around the world

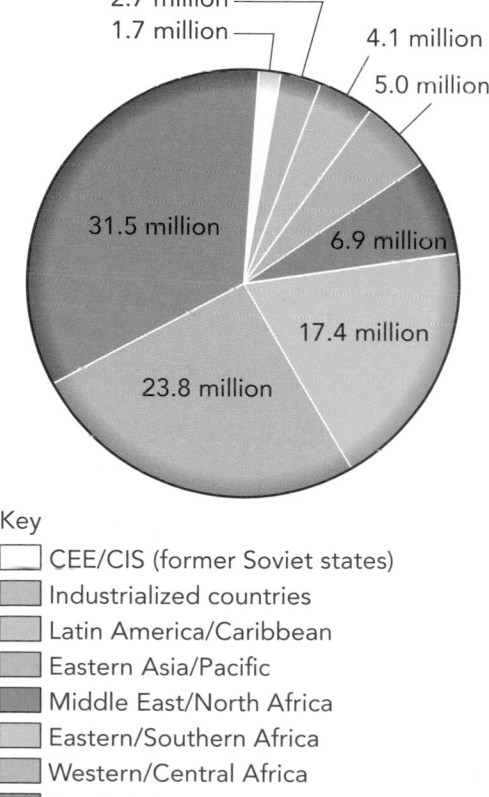

- 2.7 million
- 1.7 million
- 4.1 million
- 5.0 million
- 31.5 million
- 6.9 million
- 17.4 million
- 23.8 million

Key
- CEE/CIS (former Soviet states)
- Industrialized countries
- Latin America/Caribbean
- Eastern Asia/Pacific
- Middle East/North Africa
- Eastern/Southern Africa
- Western/Central Africa
- South Asia

How charities help

Many charities build schools or pay for teachers. Education Protection and Help for Children (EPHC) is a Nepalese charity based in Kathmandu. It offers free education to children of poor carpet-factory workers and from the streets. Its workers recruit sponsors to pay for a child's education and coordinate letters between the child and the sponsor. Other charities fund solutions to particular problems. They set up night schools in places where children have to work in the day so they can study in the evening. Many children of traveller families, who do not live permanently in one place, never go to school. Some charity workers help the parents deal with school authorities so their children can receive an education.

Celebrity school

In 2011, US TV host and actress Oprah Winfrey donated $1.5 million (£940,000) to Save the Children to rebuild the Matau Primary School in Zimbabwe. This is the home village of Tererai Trent, who talked about her passion for education and dream to rebuild the school on Oprah's show in 2009. The money was to pay workers to build and provide equipment for new classrooms and facilities and for experts to train teachers.

In Australia, Save the Children workers drive to remote regions and set up early learning centres. These centres have educational toys and games for children aged 0–5 of low-income families who would otherwise miss out. The centres help to prepare youngsters for school.

Getting girls to school

The majority of children who miss out on an education are girls. The situation is improving, but many girls still leave school or never go at all because they stay at home to work, look after younger siblings, or get married. Of around 900 million illiterate people (those unable to read) in the world, two-thirds are women. The benefits of educating a girl are huge – she is less likely to contract **HIV/AIDS**, more likely to participate in decisions that affect her community and country, to earn more, and to have healthier, educated children.

Changing minds

As well as a lack of schools, the problem is that many communities do not consider girls' education worthwhile. Workers for children's charities help communities to improve teacher training and facilities. They also devise campaigns to persuade people of its importance and work with local people to start up girls' clubs to interest girls in education. In Afghanistan, fewer than 30 per cent of girls are enrolled in schools because many families will not allow their daughters to go to places where men may see them. Therefore, workers for the charity Help The Afghan Children run an education programme to reduce the harassment of girls at school and they also run training programmes to increase the number of female teachers in the country.

Wage-boosters

An extra year of primary school boosts girls' future wages by 10 to 20 per cent.

"When I joined the training programme, I felt that I was finally given a chance to make my dreams come true. I have always wanted to be a teacher since I was a child. Very few women in Afghanistan become teachers and we need to change the system in our schools. The system is old-fashioned, cruel and includes methods like beating, insulting, punishing, and discriminating against other children".

Shukria, who participated in Save the Children's Afghanistan teacher training programme

CARE: Help Her Learn

Members of the US charity CARE run a scheme called Help Her Learn to empower and educate girls and young women. CARE adopts several different approaches to the problem. For example, some workers coordinate online and other **petitions**. They use the petitions to pressurize governments around the world to take action to prevent child marriage, which results in millions of young girls dropping out of school. Workers for the charity have also researched and developed a teaching method which enables teachers in special learning camps in India, known as UDAAN, to teach girls aged between 11 to 14 five years' worth of education in just 11 months.

The girls in the camps come from some of the poorest families in India. Camp workers use games developed by CARE experts and local educationalists. These games make learning fun, so the girls can soon read, write, and do maths and other subjects. Workers also help them to gain the confidence to think and speak for themselves. Around 9 out of 10 girls from UDAAN go on to secondary school or college. When graduates from the school find jobs and their own apartments, they serve as shining examples to people in their home villages who were not quite sure why girls needed an education.

These girls are working in a school run by a charity in Andheri, India.

Quality of education

Children who go to school do not necessarily receive a good-quality education. It may be lacking because of untrained teachers using old-fashioned teaching methods, overcrowding, or inadequate facilities. For example, in crammed classrooms with children of different ages, pupils may spend most of their time reciting memorized lines without really understanding them. Only good-quality schools keep children coming and ensure they reach their full potential. In some places, almost half of the pupils who start school drop out after less than two years.

PlayPumps

One problem many schools have is a lack of drinking water for the pupils. The PlayPump is a merry-go-round that pumps clean, safe drinking water from a deep borehole into a 2,500-litre storage tank every time children spin on it. Trevor Field, a retired advertising executive, invented the PlayPump in 2005. Since it is simple to install, some pumps are put in by volunteers, who raise funds to travel to Africa themselves to dig for water.

Trevor Field, inventor of the PlayPump, with children playing on one of his merry-go-round water pumps near Pretoria, South Africa. The pump can deliver nearly 1,400 litres of water an hour from a depth of 40 metres (130 feet). The water storage tank beside it sells advertising space to pay for maintenance of the pump. The pumps have increased attendance at many schools where they have been installed.

Computers for African Schools

Computers can help students learn, and having computer skills gives school leavers a better chance of finding jobs. The charity Computers for African Schools supplies computers to African schools and is run exclusively by volunteers. In the United Kingdom, some volunteers contact businesses and ask for unwanted but working computers. Other volunteers collect the machines, check, and repair them. Volunteers then pack the computers and deliver them to airports where airlines carry them to Africa free of charge. Volunteers in Africa install the computers and train teachers how to use them and how to teach information technology (IT) lessons.

Anne Johnson volunteered in Zambia, testing and installing software and getting computers ready for schools. This is an entry from her blog:

> We received a shipment of 450 computers from the UK at the end of August, and since then we've been VERY busy testing and installing software, and getting the computers ready for schools to collect them ... The rainy season has started early this year throughout Africa ... which was a bit of a surprise for us, and our warehouse full of computers, which has a leaky roof. I spent yesterday morning hurriedly shifting computers out of harm's way into the less leaky parts of the warehouse.

In spite of problems like this, Anne also said: "The experience has made me appreciate so much the opportunities I have had in the UK, my education, friends, and my family — all of which it is too easy to take for granted."

Volunteers fix computer parts and make sure they are in good working order before they are sent to Africa.

Opening up opportunities

Teaching is more than helping children to learn reading, writing, maths, or other academic subjects. It is also about giving young people the chance to play, take part in sport, and discover other strengths.

Many charities open up children's opportunities. Workers for the UK-based charity Youth Music provide young people with access to a wide range of music-making projects and activities. For example, musicians donate money from gigs that the charity uses to pay music teachers to run lessons or workshops. These can help children through tough times or to further musical careers. In Australia, teams of volunteers develop, advertise, and run Rotary Youth Leadership Award (RYLA) programmes that offer young people training that gives them confidence and career skills, such as adventure trips. Volunteers plan and publicize trips, select participants, run activities, and **mentor** young people. "RYLA taught me to be proud of who I am and helped me figure out what I want to do with my life. There are no limits for me now," said one youth helped by RYLA.

Beckham's gift

In 2011, international football superstar David Beckham urged fans to pay for professional-quality leather footballs and pumps for poor children. Charity workers for **UNICEF** delivered the balls to poor communities, providing children with a chance to play, exercise, and have fun. Beckham said: "I got my first football when I was very young and it was the best present I ever had. Buying one of these gifts makes a difference to a child's life."

Big Brother!

Big Brothers Big Sisters of America is a US-based charity with 370 **agencies** that support over 250,000 children a year. Money raised by the charity's fundraisers is used to pay for workers who find and support adult volunteers who want to become mentors. Then office workers called match specialists carefully match each mentor with a child who faces difficulty of some kind.

A Big Brothers Big Sisters match specialist in New York called Francy matched a young doctor called Omar with a boy called Iman. Francy's choice proved to be a big success. Iman's mum is a single mother. She works long hours, and Iman was struggling a bit at school. Volunteer big brother Omar takes Iman out for trips, such as trick-or-treating at Halloween, watches football games with him, and helps him with his homework. Now Iman is getting high grades in school and is much more confident and determined. Omar continually encourages Iman to try his hardest, no matter what the outcome, and encouraged him to start an art class to pursue his talent in drawing. "Usually when I'd do something, I would just give up if it wasn't going my way," says Iman. "Omar says you should never give up. Like, if I'm playing soccer and I'm losing, I should still play my hardest because I'll make myself better in the end."

A Big Brother mentor working on homework with a boy in a friendship initiated and funded by the Big Brothers Big Sisters of America charity.

UNICEF's Schools for Africa: Madagascar

In Madagascar, as in some other parts of Africa, around 1 in 3 children are not in school. Many of those who go to school study in overcrowded classrooms with poor-quality teaching. UNICEF teams are working with the Ministry of Education, school authorities, **non-governmental organizations (NGOs)**, local communities, and other partners to build a better future for children in Madagascar.

Getting children to school

In Madagascar, many children, especially girls, miss out on an education. This is because they have to help their families earn a living, their families cannot afford school materials, or they live in remote areas that do not have a school. UNICEF staff talk with the community about which children cannot go to school and why, and ask what the community would like to do to include them. If the problem is a lack of funds to buy books, for example, UNICEF staff may obtain money from the charity to pay for them.

In some schools, UNICEF has brought in a "big sister" programme. This is where they assist teachers in identifying young girls who may drop out of school. Then they partner these children with older girls, who take responsibility in walking their "little sisters" to school, help with homework, and build their classroom confidence.

The big sister programme

"There are far fewer drop-outs amongst the little girls of this programme ... And even the bigger girls are far more motivated. It gives them a real sense of responsibility because the big girl takes the lead."

Noro-Rakoto Joseph
UNICEF Education Officer

Technology teams

UNICEF technology teams work on providing Madagascar with the infrastructure it needs to teach the nation's children. Madagascar needs more classrooms for all the country's children. Many classrooms need rebuilding each year after they are blown down by the cyclones that hit the country regularly. The challenge for these teams is to make new classrooms cost-effective and quick to erect in remote locations.

Building innovations

A UNICEF team of technical workers developed a new technique for building classroom walls using interlocking bricks (rather like Lego) made of compressed soil, clay, and sand with lime or cement added in. Holes in the bricks can have reinforcement bars pushed through to make them stronger. This new construction method allows strong buildings, capable of withstanding cyclones, to be put up quickly. The bricks are easy for local people to make using local soils on a school site. They are dried in the air and need no wood – a scarce resource in Madagascar – or special ovens to bake, so they are cheaper, too. As UNICEF engineer Tiana Vatosoa says, "If we compare with the old bricks, it took around three months or more to do this work. But now we can make a classroom in just two months."

Children enjoying their newly built school in Mahambo, Madagascar, which was funded by UNICEF's Schools for Africa programme.

Working to improve learning

Local UNICEF employees with teaching expertise in Madagascar run teacher-training classes to help teachers to make learning fun and effective. For example, they show teachers how to make colourful cards with letters, syllables, and words on them that children put together to form a variety of words and sentences.

Another problem in Madagascar schools is that most of the books are in French rather than Malagasy, the local language that most people speak. So, in 2008, staff at UNICEF Madagascar organized a writing contest for new children's books to be written in Malagasy. UNICEF volunteers put up posters all over the country and sent postage-free envelopes to every post office so people could send in manuscripts for free. UNICEF educationalists chose 20 out of nearly 600 manuscripts to be made into story books. These have helped over 24,000 young children to learn to read or improve their literacy skills. The children have been able to read and enjoy the books at school or through lending systems organized in local schools and pre-schools.

French lessons

Madagascar was a colony of France in the past and most lessons were taught in French until 2008.

These children in a classroom in Ifaty, Madagascar, have a good chance of enjoying their school days.

Reaching children by radio

One group of UNICEF educationalists worked with children to develop a series of 15-minute radio broadcasts for primary-school children, to be aired twice a week. The programmes use friendly characters, stories, songs, skits, and games to reinforce what children learn in school and to widen their knowledge and understanding of the world. To get the most from the radio shows, teachers gather any materials that are needed and introduce the topic before each programme starts. After the programme, they ask students questions to check that they have benefited from it.

Battery-free broadcasts

To overcome the problem of schools being unable to afford radios or lacking the batteries or electricity needed to run them, UNICEF has paid for wind-up or solar-powered radios, and its workers have distributed them to more than 21,000 primary schools in Madagascar, so that children can listen to the broadcasts.

Out-of-school listening groups

In very remote areas, where children are too far from school or their school is still being completed, children can still listen to the broadcasts in one of almost 4,000 out-of-school listening groups. When 20 or so children, parents, and teachers form a group, UNICEF provides them with a wind-up or solar-powered radio. A worker from an NGO meets with the group when they gather to listen to each broadcast to ensure the families get the greatest possible benefit from the shows. The programmes not only educate the children but also help parents to understand what children do in school and why it is important.

CHILDREN'S HEALTH

Ill health stops many children attending school and affects all other aspects of their lives. Many childhood conditions have an even more serious impact – 24,000 children under the age of five die every day. Tragically, more than 90 per cent of these deaths are caused by diseases or conditions that could be prevented, such as pneumonia, measles, diarrhoea, malaria, HIV/AIDS, and complications during pregnancy and birth.

Sanitation

The majority of child deaths occur in developing countries in Africa and Asia. One cause of these deaths is a lack of **sanitation** – clean water and sewerage systems that remove human waste and keep communities clean. Water **polluted** by human or animal faeces causes illnesses such as diarrhoea and blindness, and can lead to death. Many charities raise funds to buy and install sanitation systems, to educate people about the importance of **hygiene**, and to promote community and school hand-washing campaigns.

Drinking water deaths

Over 1.5 million children every year – that's about 4,000 every day – die from illnesses caused by poor drinking water or inadequate hygiene practices.

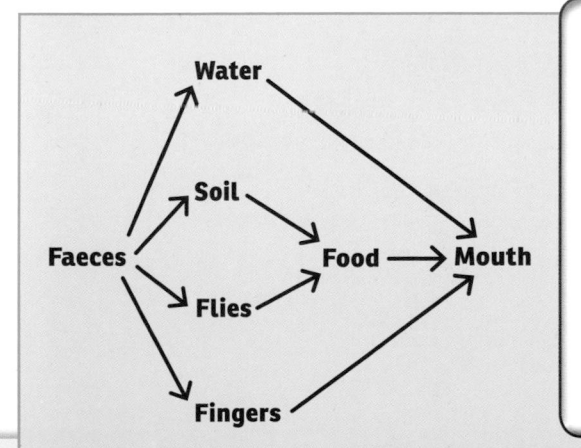

This diagram shows how particles of human faeces can get into mouths: from fingers of unwashed hands; food prepared by dirty hands; food that flies have landed on after landing on excreta; and drinking water or food from contaminated soil or water sources.

What charity workers do

Charities employ local experts or pay workers to travel to places in need to lead sanitation workshops to educate people on the importance of clean drinking water and hand-washing. They may also demonstrate how shallow wells give a clean alternative to natural open-water sources that are also used by livestock and thus cut down on child (and adult) diarrhoea. They replace school **latrine** pits with separate brick toilet blocks for girls and boys. This improves attendance in two ways. More girls come to school because they have some privacy when going to the toilet and fewer children miss school due to water-related illnesses.

Peace Corps volunteers get language, cross-cultural, and technical training so that they can live, learn, and work with communities abroad in order to help those communities find their own solutions to problems they face.

Peace Corps volunteer Kyle Borley

American Peace Corps volunteers work with a community overseas for about two years, providing technical assistance on development projects. Kyle Borley helped a secondary school in the isolated village of Barinkovka in the Ukraine. Water was available only for two to four hours every other day, and it was contaminated by rusty old pipes. Borley helped the school to work out what equipment was needed, and a local plumber fitted it, paid by the organization Water Charity. As a result, the school has a new water storage tank, water filtration system, and drinking fountain. Kyle says, "With the new filtration system and water storage container the school has been able to prepare fresh meals and provide the students with drinkable water."

Nutrition

Children need to eat well in order to grow and develop properly and to stay healthy. However, more than 178 million children around the world do not get enough to eat, and **malnutrition** causes 3.2 million child deaths each year.

Managing malnutrition

Some charity workers are doctors who run emergency wards for severely malnourished children – for example, during emergencies such as the **drought** in East Africa in 2011 that caused crop failures and severe food shortages. Other charity workers are nutritionists. Nutritionists research the types and amounts of food to give malnourished children to increase their weight safely. Scientists work on ways to fortify common foods with vitamins and minerals. Some charity workers distribute RUTF (Ready-to-Use Therapeutic Food) by ship, plane, and truck, to children who have severe malnutrition. This nutrient-rich peanut paste does not have to be mixed with water, which could be contaminated, so it is safe and quick to administer.

This chart shows the percentage of children under five years old who are underweight. In South Asia, more than 4 out of every 10 children do not get enough food.

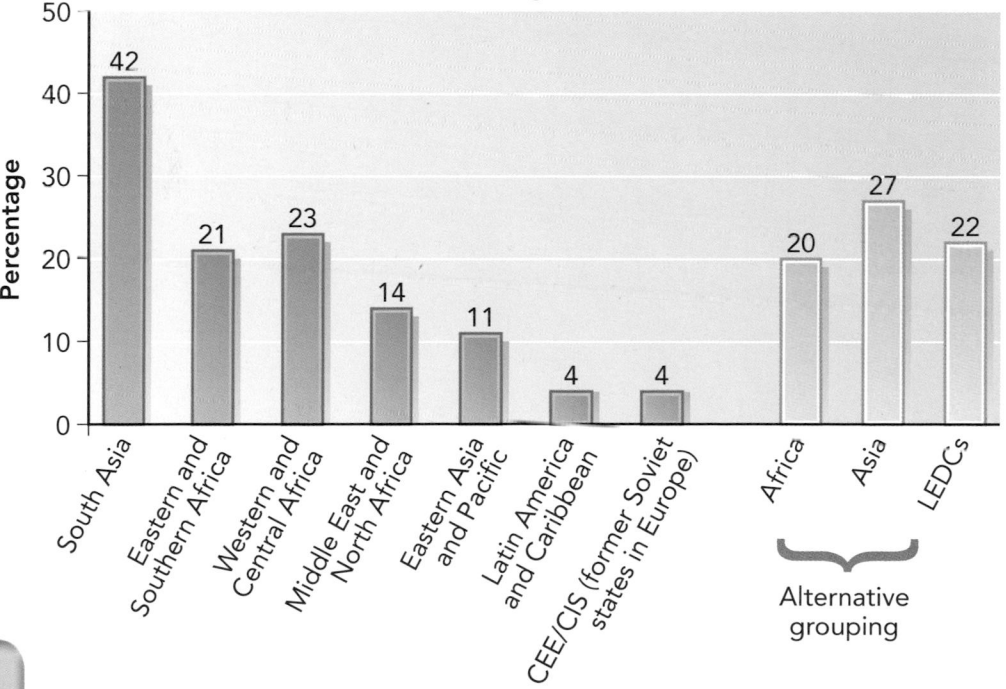

Underweight children

A day in the life of Dr Arouna

As head doctor at a Save the Children centre for malnourished children in Niger, Dr Arouna is determined to help the huge numbers of children he sees:

I've been head doctor at this centre since December 2007. I examine children and oversee the nurses, hygienists, and kitchen staff. I leave my house at 6.30 a.m. and make my rounds to see how the children were during the night, then check the medicine for the treatment at 7.30 a.m. We have new admissions every day. Sometimes I travel to pick them up. I examine them and prescribe their treatment. On a typical day it can be 8 p.m. before I leave.

An enormous number of children come to the centre in a bad state. In the worst cases, they're too weak to eat and we have to use feeding tubes. This morning, four malnourished children had to be brought from 72 kilometres [45 miles] away. Two were critical. I gave them sugared water to sustain them on the long drive. We weighed, measured, and admitted them. Acutely malnourished children are given formula for four days, and antibiotics. They should improve and move on to nutrient-rich peanut paste.

We hope we can nurse children back to health. It's the children who give me strength. I'm here because of them – I have a boy of my own who's six months old. It's a pleasure for the whole team to see a child recover.

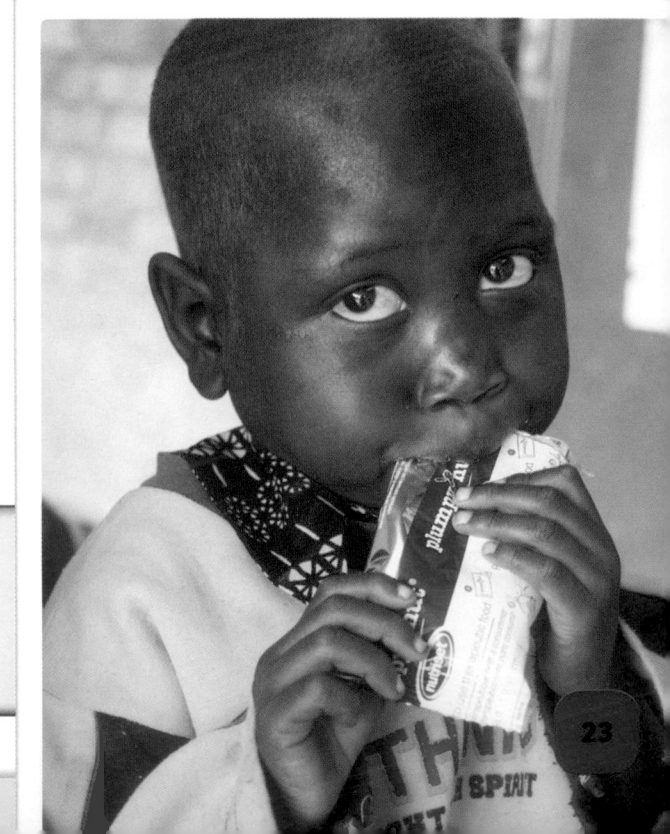

This child in Rwanda is eating nutrient-rich peanut paste.

Informing families

Another cause of malnutrition is a lack of understanding of nutrition. Some charity workers write reports and attend meetings to pressurize governments to make nutrition information a key part of their national policies and budgets. Others work directly with families to provide them with good information on nutrition and the resources to help them achieve it. For example, some charity workers visit communities to distribute seeds and farm tools among families. Other workers hold training classes for school cooks and families to discuss the range of vitamins, minerals, and other nutrients children need.

Tackling childhood obesity

In some **more economically developed countries (MEDCs)**, a third of children are overweight and risk developing serious health problems, such as heart disease. Some children's charities help by providing healthy food choices and exercise. Many poorer families cannot afford fresh food or do not live close to shops selling it. The US charity San Antonio Food Bank grows or collects donations of fresh food and distributes it to children and families. Turning Wheels For Kids is a US-based charity staffed by volunteers who collect funds, and purchase and assemble bikes. They distribute them to a medical centre that works with overweight children so that they can cycle for exercise.

Volunteering is great!

"I had the opportunity to volunteer with the San Antonio Food Bank this past Saturday morning. I helped in the garden in pulling weeds out around the tomato plants ... I plan on volunteering more of my time at the San Antonio Food Bank. Any volunteering is great for yourself and for others!"

Marissa Rew

Working for CINI India

Dr Samir Chaudhuri set up the charity Children in Need Institute (CINI) in Kolkata in 1974. He explains:

> I started working as a **paediatrician** [children's doctor] in the **slums** of Kolkata in 1974, treating malnourished children with low immunity who were overcome with diarrhoea and chest infections. Many of them returned within a few weeks with the same illness, as the root causes of the problem had not been addressed. It soon became clear that malnutrition was playing a deadly role.

Chaudhuri began with a small Saturday clinic advising mothers on nutrition and treating children. Today, some CINI workers educate women and especially pregnant mothers. They visit and train teams of women to run training classes for other women from their local community about what, when, and how much to feed their babies. In some traditional cultures, mothers in families where limited food is available often eat a smaller share of it than men and boys. The community workers also explain the importance of mothers having a good intake of vitamins and minerals while they are feeding babies. Training local workers to educate families is of huge benefit because they understand local situations and can engage successfully with the women.

Mothers of malnourished children help to prepare meals on a CINI ward in India.

Diseases and disability

Charity workers tackle childhood diseases and help children with disabilities or life-threatening illnesses in many ways.

Vaccinations

Vaccination against potentially dangerous childhood diseases is the most cost-effective lifesaver for children. While some countries offer children vaccinations for free, in others, hundreds of thousands of poor children die from vaccine-preventable diseases every year. Charity workers work in different ways to deliver more vaccinations. For example, some are nurses, doctors, and pharmacists who travel in mobile health clinics to remote places or slums to give children the vaccinations they need. Other charity workers source and distribute motorbikes to health workers so they can reach the poorest children in remote areas. Some provide **solar panels** to power fridges and spare parts for fridges that store vaccination medicines. They build, refurbish (repair), and support health clinics in the poorest and most remote areas, so children can come to be vaccinated.

In 2010, Red Cross volunteers from around the world flew to Haiti to give people injections after an earthquake in Haiti disrupted the government's vaccination campaign.

Supplying medicines to remote places

Médecins Sans Frontières (Doctors Without Borders) provides medical care to people in need in remote and often dangerous places. Many different kinds of people volunteer for the charity, not just doctors.

Conor Prenderville trained in business and management and worked in the building industry for several years before he joined the charity. Prenderville is a supply logistician. His job is to source the correct medicines from suppliers around the world and organize for them to be transported to mobile clinics in out of the way places. He started in Chad. "We had a lot of emergencies," he says. "They were mainly problems of malnutrition, but also some cholera. The mission grew from one to eight projects in the time that I was there, so we saw a lot of turbulence."

From Chad, he travelled to the Haitian capital Port-au-Prince to work with a team dealing with a cholera outbreak. Then he was part of a team providing free mobile clinics to towns in the Bolívar region in Colombia, where armed groups were fighting and people were trapped in remote places. Here, the team treated thousands of patients. It is Prenderville's skills in supply management – his ability to keep stock of everything from bars of soap to vaccines – that are vital to the success of every mission. "The benefits that you can bring to people are so real," he says. "At the end of the day, I know that our teams save lives every day – many, many lives."

What is Médecins Sans Frontières?

Médecins Sans Frontières (MSF) is an international medical **humanitarian** organization created by doctors and journalists in France in 1971. Today, MSF provides aid in nearly 60 countries to people whose survival is threatened by violence, neglect, or catastrophe, primarily due to armed conflict, epidemics, malnutrition, exclusion from health care, or natural disasters. On any one day, more than 27,000 committed individuals representing dozens of nationalities can be found providing assistance to people caught in crises around the world.

HIV/AIDS education

AIDS (acquired immune deficiency syndrome) is a medical condition caused by HIV. This is a virus that weakens the immune system so people catch and die from common diseases more easily. It is passed between people through bodily fluids, including blood, semen, and mother's milk. Some charity workers give out drugs that can control and slow the progress of the disease (though not cure it) or medicines that can prevent newborns from contracting HIV/AIDS from their mothers.

Some workers teach young people how to protect themselves against HIV. Charity workers meet youth groups to find out how best to raise awareness. For example, they ensure that leaflets avoid using complicated medical terms. Workers must also take into account the sensitivity of local cultures to such subjects as sex and drug use. In some places, teachers and youth leaders do not have experience dealing with these issues, so trainers from charities help them to find ways of discussing the issues. Workers from UNICEF collaborated with MTV to make "Shuga", a three-part TV soap drama about young adults living in Nairobi, broadcast in Kenya and Zambia in 2009. It covered issues such as HIV testing, unprotected sex, and relationships, and was accompanied by radio and internet campaigns.

HIV infections

In 2009, globally there were 890,000 new HIV infections among young people aged 15–24.

This family is benefiting from a UNICEF programme that supplies mosquito nets to prevent them from contracting malaria.

Making life better

While some charity workers deal with medicine and treatment, others help children with disabilities or long-term health problems to make their lives easier and more enjoyable. Some charity workers organize equipment such as touch-screen computers or powered wheelchairs to help disabled children become more independent. Charity volunteers may be ordinary families who regularly take a disabled child out swimming, playing in the park, enjoying football, or for another activity. They may have the child come to stay with them to give the child and his or her carers a break. Some charity workers provide therapy. For example, taking children with special educational needs and disabilities horse riding can bring pleasure and build confidence.

Disability fact

One in every 10 children around the world copes with a disability.

Spreading sunshine

The Sunshine Foundation of Canada grants wishes to children with severe disabilities and life-threatening illnesses. It might help them meet a sports hero, visit a foreign country, or have a gift like a specially adapted bicycle. Jen Visscher worked for the charity as a National Dream Fulfillment Coordinator, working with families and healthcare professionals to make a child's dream come true. This involved booking trips, coordinating celebrity meetings, and ordering gifts, and also training and working with volunteers. Jen says, "I have thoroughly enjoyed the conversations, the laughter, the tears and everything in between in working on ... children's dreams."

ABUSE AND NEGLECT

Some charities are dedicated to helping children who suffer physical or sexual abuse, neglect, or other forms of cruelty. This is an especially challenging field, because charity workers often have to balance the children's rights with the rights of families.

Protecting children

Volunteer counsellors for charities such as ChildLine in the United Kingdom or ChildHelp in the United States provide advice and support on free phone or online services 24 hours a day. Calls are confidential (kept secret) so young people can talk freely about their concerns. Other workers build websites with information young people can access to find out about issues such as bullying and abuse. Charity **social workers** visit schools to talk to children about abuse and bullying, how to protect themselves, and where to find help if they need it.

Young people just want to talk

"A lot of the time, young callers just want to talk to someone. Often they are calling before they have run away while they are considering it. We would try to encourage them to talk to someone – either at school or someone in their family. We'd also tell them about social services or a local **drop-in centre**, or other helplines. They need to know that they have options and people they can talk to."

Jill Taylor, a volunteer on the Runaway Helpline

Reports of abuse

In 2009 in the United States, approximately 3.3 million child-abuse reports and allegations were made, involving an estimated 6 million children.

Meet Alex – Host on the ChildLine Message Board

Alex works on the ChildLine website, where young people share information and experiences with each other, such as worries or questions about abuse, bullying, and self harm. The idea for the message boards was to provide a way for users to offer each other peer support. Alex says: "I love the way users on ChildLine are so supportive! It's very rare that a question goes unanswered and posters give up their own time to help support others. A lot of the time other members of the community answer questions before I see them and do a great job!"

Alex works on everything message-board related on the ChildLine website: "I keep the message boards tidy – I close threads if users ask me to, remove duplicate messages, and create the **sticky threads** you see at the top of some of the message boards. I also pass on information from within ChildLine to the community and feedback from the community back to ChildLine. For example, recently I have been working closely with ChildLine's participation team to help represent the views on the message boards to the Minister for Children and Families [who advises the government on children's issues such as health, disability, and child centres]. Oh, and I also get to do lots of testing on new versions of the site, which is harder work than you might think!"

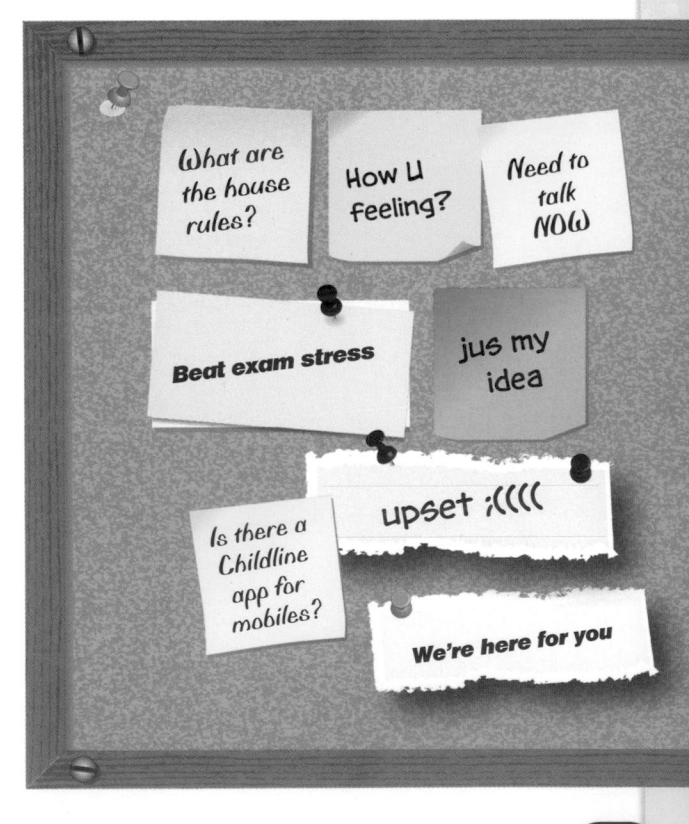

Exploitation

Sexual exploitation of children ranges from an older person coercing a child into a sexual relationship, to serious organized crime, such as **child trafficking**. Some sexual exploitation project workers go into schools to teach vulnerable young people to protect themselves. For example, they suggest avoiding activities that put them at increased risk, such as drug-taking, and explain how abusers can manipulate young people. Barnardo's is calling for a dedicated government minister in the United Kingdom to be given responsibility for tackling all child sexual exploitation crimes.

"Turn Around" advertising campaign

Barnardo's commissioned a TV advert shown in 2011 called "Turn Around". This focused on a young girl who was sexually exploited and trapped in a situation with a man she could not escape from, before Barnardo's intervened. To make the advert, Barnardo's spoke to young victims of sexual exploitation who had been helped by Barnardo's. This helped to make the advert as realistic as possible. TV campaigns like this are expensive, but marketing officers argue that they encourage people to donate money and tell vulnerable children who they can call for help.

When homeless children have to sleep on the streets, they can be vulnerable to exploitation.

Street children

Many children leave home because of violence, **substance abuse**, or parental neglect, and end up living on the streets. Some have no home because their parents have died from AIDS. Street children, wherever they are, are vulnerable not only to cold, hunger, and disease, but also to other adults who abuse or exploit them. They are also in danger of injury from gangs, and many turn to drugs, glue sniffing, or alcohol as a means of escape.

Street children in the USA

There are 1.3 million street children in the United States, not counting children who were forced out of their homes, abandoned by the foster-care system, or are part of a homeless family. The average age of a homeless person in the United States is just nine!

Outreach workers

Many charities train volunteers or employees as **outreach workers**, who "reach out" to street children. They take time to get to know them and find out the children's needs and what they themselves might find helpful. It takes time and effort to gain the confidence of street children. They are often distrustful of any adults because of past abuse or exploitation.

Some charities employ former street children as outreach workers. They know how life on the street feels and can relate to street children in a way they understand. Many children living on the streets are forced into a life of crime in order to survive. The vast majority of street children steal in order to live, and many become prostitutes. Others resort to begging to get enough income to buy food.

Helping street children in Mexico

Nikita Holden is a volunteer for Casa Alianza Mexico, which seeks to help children living on the street.

> Each day the team meets to plan the areas they will travel to and discuss any important cases ... Once the plan has been made the team sets off at 8.00 a.m. equipped with first aid kits, games, and footballs. They travel large distances to the south and north of the city, by bus, metro, or on foot in hope of finding the children...
>
> Most of the children look forward to the team's arrival as it is a chance to break their daily routine of taking the powerful solvent "activo" and the other harsh realities of life on the street ... Once the team has said their hellos to the children, they then set about to encourage the children to stop taking drugs in order that they can play a game, be it playing cards ... board games, or playing football.
>
> However, the street outreach team offers so much more ... than just a chance to play a game; they are continually offering advice on how they can begin the transition from the streets... They also establish *un plan de vida*, a life plan with the children that seeks to set realistic and obtainable goals that the children can work towards with the help, support, and guidance of the entire Casa Alianza Mexico organization.

Supporting street children

Some charities fund mobile units that drive out to areas where street children gather, such as under bridges. They employ van drivers to take nurses and other staff to provide them with medicine, first aid, food, and clothes. Some charities fund day care or reception centres, where children can drop in every day. Workers here cook meals and give classes and training workshops. Counsellors are on hand to talk to children about their reasons for living on the street and offer advice and comfort.

Running refuges

Some charity workers run refuges where children can stay overnight to escape dangers on the streets. For example, the Australian charity SunnyKids provides around 22,500 nights of emergency accommodation for children across the states of Queensland and Victoria every year. Other project workers may recruit, train, and supervise "hosts" – couples and families who give street children shelter in their own homes for a few weeks, until project workers can review their situation – or the children may move into temporary shelters. Most refuges or centres also have counsellors who work with children to help them recover from **addiction**, and social workers who try to enable children to return to the family home or find them more permanent sheltered accommodation. Some project workers run long-term residential centres where children can stay until they are old enough to settle into a home of their own.

Street children may live in abandoned buildings, cardboard boxes, parks, or on the street itself. These young homeless boys living inside cardboard boxes are in Cairo, Egypt.

Getting kids off the streets

Camila Batmanghelidjh has lots of experience working with children. She completed a Master's degree in the philosophy of counselling and psychotherapy, spent two years studying child psychology, and took a course in art therapy.

She began the youth charity Kids Company in 1996 when she opened her first drop-in centre in some disused railway arches in South London. Young people could walk in off the streets to escape their problems outside. On the first day, local teenage boys ransacked the centre with bricks and knives, but Batmanghelidjh did not call the police. She just kept opening her doors. Soon, the area's most troubled and vulnerable teenagers were pouring in, seeking her help. In her own words:

> The fascinating element in all these children's lives is the absence of a functioning parental figure. If you don't have a parent there is no food in the house, no one washes your clothes or organizes socializing for you, you don't get taken to the GP, the dentist, or the optician. You live in chaos. The assumption is that if you are seven years old, there is an adult who can refer you to social services. But these children do not have that adult in their lives and they have no access to help. Back when I started, there were people saying to me that what I was trying to achieve wasn't possible and that it wouldn't work. They just thought that I was an eccentric who loves kids, and they became very preoccupied with the way I look and dress.

Camila Batmanghelidjh founded the London-based charity Kids Company to provide practical, emotional, and educational support to vulnerable inner-city children.

Wraparound care

These days, Kids Company helps 12,000 children, operating through two street-level centres and a therapy house in South London, a drop-in centre in North London, and therapeutic and social-work services in over 30 schools. Many young people come to the Arches II centre six days a week, where a team of social workers, youth offending workers, teachers, employment advisers, **psychologists**, nurses, **alternative health therapists**, art therapists, and a doctor try to meet all their practical and emotional needs.

The team offers practical support, including three nutritional meals a day, housing, and health care. They help to educate young people and to address emotional and behavioural difficulties, such as through art therapy. They also give children the chance to have fun. The aim is to first meet each young person's practical needs, then help them to work through the trauma many have experienced through physical and sexual abuse, and then assist them to identify interests and develop aspirations for the future. Kids Company's work can bring them into contact with dangerous people. As Camila says:

> My staff and I are working in a very risky environment and we are at risk from the wider communities we work in. When we first started, the firearms were in the hands of the drug dealers and they would only use them to mind their business. Now they are in the hands of 15- and 16-year-olds. It's a different ball game. We have hired extra security to stand at our gates in bulletproof vests ... But my kids have lived this life, every day, as little children. The least I can do as an adult is live it with them 14 hours a day.

Numbers of neglected children

Kids Company reports that each year in the United Kingdom over 550,000 cases of child abuse and neglect are referred to social services, but due to the strain on resources, over 90 per cent of children are left without support.

Child labour

Around 215 million children worldwide are engaged in some form of labour (work) every day. Some help their families on farms or in shops. Others work in poor conditions. They may make bricks, work in mines, break stones, or suffer abuse when they work as servants and cleaners in homes. Many of these children are forced to work; some have been abducted. They are denied an education and a normal childhood. Some are confined and beaten, and denied the right to go home to their families.

For charity workers, a key factor in preventing child labour is raising awareness of the damage it does. They explain to parents who themselves worked from a young age how education can benefit their children. Charity workers also make it clear how working at a young age can affect children physically in the long term. For example, lungs are damaged by dust and fumes, backs are malformed through carrying heavy loads, and eyesight is ruined by working in poor light.

Child Protection Committees

UNICEF workers help local people to form Village Child Protection Committees that encourage people to stop child labour. Committee members persuade families to enrol their children in school and visit the family regularly afterwards to check that the children continue to attend school.

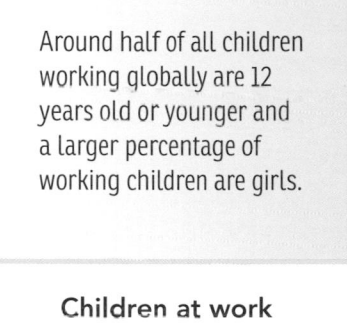

Around half of all children working globally are 12 years old or younger and a larger percentage of working children are girls.

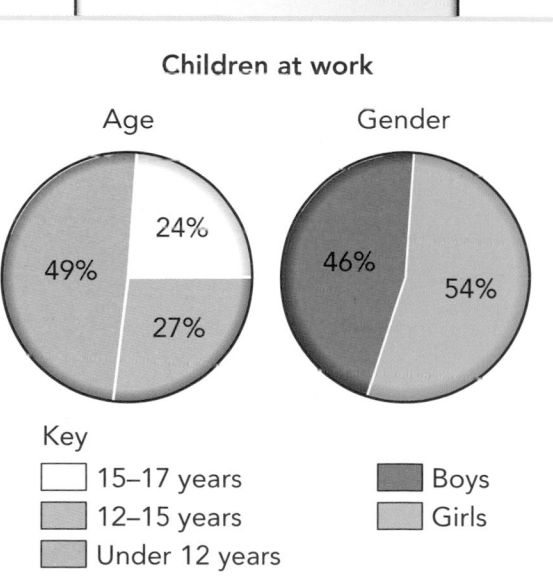

Children at work

Age

24%
49%
27%

Gender

46%
54%

Key

15–17 years	Boys
12–15 years	Girls
Under 12 years	

Braulio's escape from mining in Peru

Braulio had been working in La Rinconada mine since he was very small, crushing stones and carrying heavy loads of ore. At 13, he says, "One day I didn't feel well, I was very tired and fell down a few times while I was working. At the exit from the mine my barrow overturned and all the ore fell out. The captain was watching me. He kicked me hard because of this."

Braulio had heard on the radio about a CARE charity project working to prevent child labour in the mines, so he called a project worker for help. "They came to the mine and talked to the mine manager, and he was **sanctioned**. After that I only worked for one more month, helping to take care of the owner's warehouse."

Braulio, his brothers, and their father went to CARE meetings. Braulio continues, "We learnt that working was not good for us. I had aches and pains, sometimes we didn't eat well, and it was difficult to go to school and study. Now we are in a better situation. We know more and want to move ahead and be successful in our lives." Braulio's father now realizes that his children's education is vital. "My father was very grateful and told them that from now on only he would work, and that we could devote ourselves to school."

This young boy is hard at work digging copper in a mine in the Democratic Republic of Congo. Children as young as eight years old work here in dangerous conditions and a few of the miners are killed every month.

Forcing policy changes

Around 60 per cent of child labourers in the world work on farms. Most are unpaid because they work with their family. Many charity workers try to protect these child labourers by influencing governments. For example, workers for the charity International Initiative to End Child Labor (IIECL) investigate children working in the fields in the United States and use this information to push for stronger child labour laws.

Saving children from the fields

Joanna Ewart-James works at Anti-Slavery International, a charity that campaigns to end slavery and forced labour. She says: "I talk to companies to raise their awareness about possible slavery and forced labour in their supply chains, and also campaign to raise public awareness of the issues." Joanna is involved in a campaign to get high-street fashion retailers to boycott cotton made in Uzbekistan, where the government forces tens of thousands of young children to harvest cotton every year. "I think people would be very shocked if they knew that the T-shirt they are wearing was made with cotton picked by children in forced labour." Joanna has organized meetings to encourage the **European Commission** to put pressure on the Uzbek government.

Children who work on farms are four times more likely to die because of the equipment they handle.

Sweatshops

Sweatshops are factories where workers are paid low wages and work in cramped and often dangerous conditions. They make items such as shoes, clothing, footballs, rugs, and toys so the factory owner can sell these things cheaply. Sweatshop workers are often children – around 75 per cent of Pakistan's carpet weavers are girls under 14.

This does not happen only in **less economically developed countries (LEDCs)**. Although laws prevent child labour in countries such as the United Kingdom, United States, and Australia, many children still work alongside their parents doing **piecework** – a small amount of money is paid per item produced. Child labour is hard to fight because the cause is poverty. Children work so their families can survive.

Improving families' wages

Some charity workers provide centres where working children can receive an education and the hope of raising themselves out of poverty. Others train the parents of child labourers – for example, to teach them new skills or to help them start their own businesses.

Some charity workers help families to organize funds to pay off debts, so their children no longer have to work. Other charity workers deliver seeds and farm equipment so families can grow food more efficiently and do not need to rely on child labour. Helping parents to increase family incomes means fewer children have to work.

The price of fashion

Typically, the worker who made a cheap fashion garment will receive between 0.5 and 4 per cent of the average price the garment sells for!

Child trafficking

Child trafficking is when children are removed from their homes and families, transported elsewhere, within a country or overseas, and forced into sexual, domestic, sweatshop, or field labour. They are treated as slaves, deprived of family and education, and often abused. At least 1.2 million children are trafficked every year and the problem is not isolated to LEDCs. Victims are also trafficked into countries such as the United States and the United Kingdom.

Empowering people against the traffickers

Families are often unaware of the dangers of trafficking, and are misled into sending their child to live with a friend, relative, or stranger believing that education or good work opportunities await their son or daughter. Some charity workers visit communities to educate parents about the perils of these arrangements, and to teach them how to avoid such traps. Sometimes children themselves leave because they may be under pressure from their families to find work to help support the family, and there may not be work available locally. Other charity workers help young people to escape their captors, provide short-term shelters and medical care to victims of trafficking, and try to reunite them with their families.

Training manual

UNICEF pays researchers and experts to constantly update the training manual it produces about how to fight child trafficking. This keeps people in governments, NGOs, and international agencies on top of developments in the trade and helps to train people how to plan for and how to fight trafficking of children.

Blue Dragon rescues trafficked children

In October 2002, an Australian teacher called Michael Brosowski arrived in Hanoi, Vietnam to teach English at the university. In his spare time, he gave lessons to kids on the streets. In 2004, he left work to start the Blue Dragon charity to help more children. Since 2005, Blue Dragon has worked with children who had been trafficked to Ho Chi Minh City to work on the streets or in factories. Michael and his workers find ways to rescue the children and help them return home. He says: "Child by child, we've got to work out what we can do and what they need. And we've also got to be careful that if the child has a family, that the family is as involved as possible."

One child the charity helped is Tran. Traffickers took Tran from his village in central Vietnam to Ho Chi Minh City. They promised Tran's mother that he would go to school during the day and work just a few hours at night in a shop, but there was no school and no shop. Tran was forced to sell flowers to tourists throughout the night. The work was dangerous, tiring, and unpaid. Blue Dragon staff rescued 13-year-old Tran from the streets and took him home to his family. Because of the danger that the traffickers would come back for him, Blue Dragon workers later took Tran to the charity's residential home in Hanoi. Tran is doing very well at school, visits his parents every school holiday, and is looking forward to attending university.

Charities may run campaigns asking people to sign petitions against child trafficking.

43

CHILDREN AND CONFLICT

Many wars are fought within countries, and most battles are fought in streets and villages. This is why more than 90 per cent of war victims today are civilians, not soldiers, at least half of whom are children. Children are injured or killed by war, displaced (forced to move away) from the communities where they live, separated from families, and forced to join in combat as child soldiers.

Saving lives

During conflict, millions more children die from lack of food and the destruction of health services, water systems, and sanitation than the actual fighting. Some charity workers distribute emergency aid such as food, water, and shelters. Health workers and paediatricians tend wounds and give vaccinations against diseases such as cholera that can spread when health systems break down. Charities also employ counsellors and psychologists who talk to children to help them to deal with the trauma of losing loved ones.

Reuniting families

In the chaos of war, children may become separated from their families. Some charity workers take registers of **refugee** children when they arrive in a camp. They locate and interview foster parents within the camp to care for unaccompanied child refugees. Then they work to reunite the children with their missing relatives. They circulate posters in public places with the children's photos, in the hope that a relative or friend of the family will recognize them.

Out of school

More than 37 million children cannot go to school because they live in countries affected by conflict – that's over half the children out of school worldwide.

Landmines

Landmines are weight-triggered explosive devices put on the land during wars, which remain dangerous for years afterwards. Almost 50 per cent of victims are children, who are killed, blinded, or disabled by landmines. Workers from charities such as Help The Afghan Children (HTAC) teach children to look out for landmines. Health workers fit children who have lost an arm or a leg with a **prosthetic** (artificial limb), to help them lead normal lives again.

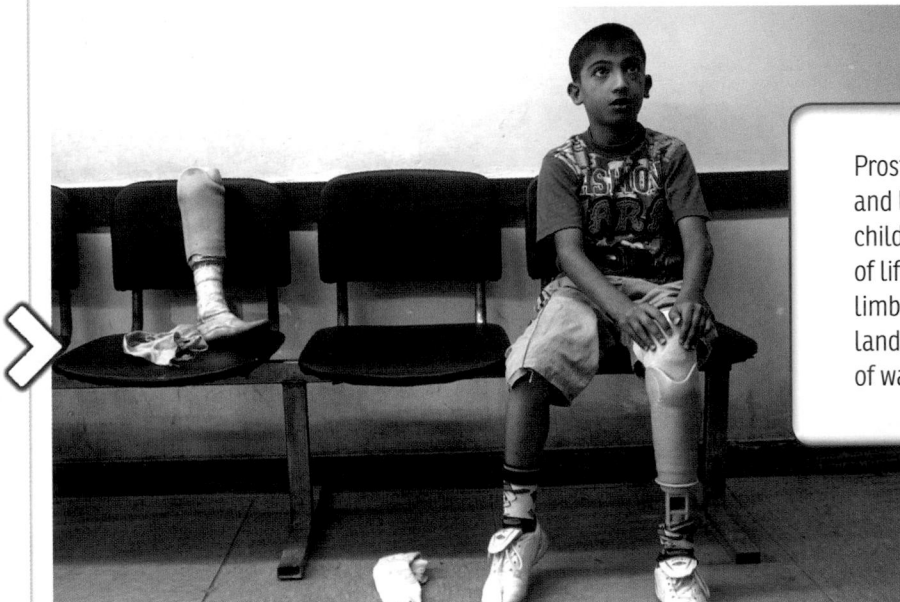

Prosthetic arms and legs can give children a new lease of life when they lose limbs to bombs and landmines in times of war.

Running refugee camps

Conflict has forced millions of children and families to flee within their own country or escape to other countries as refugees. As well as supplying tents and huts, mattresses, blankets, and kitchen equipment, workers from charities such as Oxfam work with refugees to build structures such as latrines and train refugees to maintain them. Charities set up temporary schools for refugee children and provide teachers or help to train adult refugees to take classes. Workers also set up child-friendly spaces, where children can play. They try to staff these spaces with people from the local community, who are familiar with local customs, to help children begin to recover from their experiences and leave parents free to find work.

BEING A HEALTH WORKER IN A REFUGEE CAMP

Julia Moore is Oxfam's public health promoter, promoting good hygiene and preventing the outbreak of disease in the Bishop Ferguson Centre refugee camp in Liberia. She says:

> The focus of my work is on education, working with community members to ensure knowledge, participation, and prevention. We focus on very basic things like showing people how to use the latrines properly or making sure everyone washes their hands after going to the toilet: basic things that make a huge difference.

Julia has been a refugee herself, so she knows what life in a camp is like: "There's one little boy here who likes to keep me company and be my 'assistant'. On the days that he doesn't turn up I know it's because his clothes are being washed. He came with only the clothes he was wearing, and when they're being washed he doesn't have anything else to wear, so he stays in his tent."

Having experience of being a refugee helps people connect to her:

> I've worked in Sudan and Pakistan as well, but being here educating people and providing information and assistance to refugees in my own country makes me really happy. Some people here can't believe that I was a refugee myself. I tell them: "I walked on the same path as you to get where I am today." I share my story with them to try to give them hope for the future and help them take action to make their own lives better.

Counting child soldiers

It is estimated that hundreds of thousands of children under the age of 18 serve in government forces or armed rebel groups. Some are as young as eight years old.

Child soldiers

In war zones in troubled countries, armies recruit children as soldiers. Some are kidnapped, while others join for protection from the violence or to be sure of regular meals, clothing, or medical attention. Some are used to fight, others as porters, cooks, or spies. They may be sent into battle as scouts or as decoys to draw enemy fire. Child soldiers are small and eat little food, and modern weapons are light and easy enough for them to use. Many are killed, while survivors are often physically and emotionally damaged for life. Often they cannot return home because communities reject them, and having missed school, it is hard to find work.

Helping child soldiers

Charity workers work in different ways to help child soldiers. They investigate where child soldiers are being used and work for their release. They help children to recover from the emotional and physical damage caused. They educate children to help them catch up on missed schoolwork and train children so they have a chance of finding work. Some charity workers help to reunite child soldiers with their families and help to settle them back into their former communities.

Hundreds of thousands of children under 18 serve in government forces or armed rebel groups. Some are as young as eight years old.

War Child projects for child soldiers

War Child is an international charity that protects children living in the world's most dangerous war zones. It was founded in 1993 by British filmmakers Bill Leeson and David Wilson, when they returned from filming the war in former Yugoslavia. Shocked by what they had seen, they raised enough money to return later that year with a convoy and mobile bakery to help provide for the children affected by the conflict. Today War Child runs projects in several countries, and has become a family of humanitarian organizations working together to help children affected by war.

War Child

"War Child is one of the world's most important charities."
> Chris Martin, from the band Coldplay

Meeting emotional needs

Many child soldiers have nightmares or develop depression, and they experience outbursts of anger, difficulty concentrating, or a lack of confidence. War Child workers devise creative teaching methods and workshops and teach social workers in war zones how to lead the workshops to help children to deal with these problems. The I DEAL scheme, devised by workers from War Child Holland, is a carefully planned series of activities that use music, dance, acting, sports, and group discussions to help children learn to cope with their experiences, express their emotions, and build their confidence. By learning to play again, children are also able to escape the difficulties of their daily lives for a while.

Helping children help themselves

War Child workers treat rescued child soldiers as survivors and not just victims. They help children to use their abilities and skills to change their own lives and to help each other. They do this by running sports clubs, child and youth clubs, and other activities to encourage child soldiers to interact together. Sharing their experiences, ideas, and problems helps the young people. It helps them to rebuild their own identity and to learn about building cooperation and trust – skills they may have lost during their war experiences.

Film projects

War Child is also involved in film and music projects. For example, staff from the charity helped to develop the award-winning film *The Silent Army* (2009), which was based on real-life experiences of former child solders who took part in War Child programmes. War Child offered knowledge and expertise about child soldiers in Africa to create a script that was as authentic as possible so that the film would raise public awareness of the issue of child soldiers.

It costs money and it takes time to help child soldiers. This volunteer is collecting donations of cash at a War Child Benefit Concert held in the United States.

LOOKING TO THE FUTURE

The people who work for children's charities do a wide range of different jobs, all of which contribute to the wider aim of protecting and caring for children. One of the key issues is helping children and their families or carers achieve long-term stability. Sometimes short-term or emergency aid is vital, such as a supply of food in a drought or rebuilding a school that has been bombed. But for all charities, the ultimate aim is to help people to help themselves.

Involving individuals

The first step for many charities is to employ workers to talk to the children about what the problem is and find out what changes they would like to see happen. To ensure the voices of children are heard, much of the work charities do is supported by the media – such as the internet and TV and especially the radio, which in LEDCs is often the medium that reaches people most easily.

Developments in technology and the media, such as blogging, encourage public debate and give young people an opportunity to make their voices heard and to be involved in the discussion of issues that directly affect them. Involving people on the ground in planning means that any solutions charities help to put into place are more likely to be successful, appropriate for the culture of the people involved, and have long-lasting impact.

Uniting against poverty

The Global Call to Action Against Poverty is a growing alliance that brings together trade unions, NGOs, youth movements, community groups, and others. The group calls for action from world leaders to meet their promises to end poverty and inequality and it includes charities such as Save the Children and UNICEF.

Big issues

Children are part of families, schools, and other communities, so when a charity works on any project to help a community, it is helping to care for and protect children, too. Charities often tackle wider issues, such as poverty. Across the world there are children living in poverty, mostly from LEDCs but also in MEDCs, such as the United Kingdom and the United States, where there are some children living in damp, dirty, overcrowded housing without enough money for food. To address major issues such as poverty, which affect children and others, charities may join forces.

Charities that are working to combat poverty or big issues like sanitation for whole communities are also helping children. Because of poverty and a lack of access to basic services such as water, these African children have to walk kilometres every day, often missing school in order to help their families during times of drought.

Future projects

Charities also employ researchers who investigate factors that will impact on children's well-being in the future. They give these reports to charity officers, who write proposals for new projects. Many researchers are looking at the impacts of climate change because they cause more drought and therefore greater food shortages. The poorest children suffer the most from these problems. Planning in advance and doing all they can to help people overcome their poverty now, is one way to help children in the future.

Making children's voices heard

UNICEF has run a number of projects to help to uphold young people's right to a voice. In 2009, the charity sent teenage representatives from G8 countries (see box below) to a young people's summit in Italy, called the Junior 8 (J8), to discuss their concerns about global issues. The charity teamed up with a national TV channel, which ran a report about the J8 in a news bulletin. It encouraged young people to enter UNICEF's J8 competition to win a place at the summit, which involved producing videos or written work based on the J8 topics: the environment and climate change, and HIV and AIDS. The J8 summit included winning teams from G8 countries together with participants from eight non-G8 countries – including China, Brazil, India, and South Africa – to send a message to leaders that children from all over the world are equally affected by G8 decisions.

What is the G8?

The G8 is a group of eight countries – Russia and seven of the world's rich nations: France, Germany, Italy, Japan, the United Kingdom, United States, and Canada. The **European Union** is also represented. The countries' leaders get together to discuss global problems and what action to take to solve them. The leaders of the eight countries take it in turns to be president of the G8. Members meet at an annual summit that is held in the country that has that year's presidency.

Taking young people's opinions into account

Four teenagers from London were at the J8 event. They helped to write a declaration to world leaders to ensure they take young people's views into account. In 2009, their recommendations included reducing greenhouse gas emissions (the gases that are making the earth warmer), ensuring a quality education for all children, and reducing poverty in LEDCs.

The J8 recommendations

"[The J8] was a great opportunity, getting to meet the world leaders ... I got to put our views across and I think they listened to me. [Prime Minister] Gordon Brown introduced me to all the leaders, including [US President] Barack Obama. They agreed that our declaration was better than theirs because it was way shorter and the ideas were much better."

Mellika Myers, aged 16

As well as putting their views directly to heads of state and government, the J8 team did blogs and TV reports to engage other young people throughout the United Kingdom. "Every year we get the winning team to blog about what they're doing in the run up to the summit, to make sure that they're including other young people's opinions," comments Jessica Wright, Youth Web Editor at UNICEF UK. "I think as years go by, they're starting to take more and more notice and realize how important it is that young people's opinions are taken into account."

Listen up! Junior 8 Summit participants pose in front of a giant papier mache ear in Rome at the G8 Summit in Italy, 2009. The J8 has been running every year since 2005.

VOLUNTEERING

Even small actions can make a difference, and volunteering to help others is a good way to make that difference. For many volunteering jobs, you do not need any experience, special skills, or qualifications. There are lots of simple but hugely important jobs to do, like collecting donations or handing out leaflets for which you just need to be willing to give your time, energy, and enthusiasm!

Being a volunteer helps you, too

Volunteering can be great fun – running a fundraising party or taking part in a sponsored bike ride can be really satisfying. Volunteering is also a great way to meet new people who, like you, want to give something back to their community. Many volunteers also find that their work increases their confidence and boosts their teamwork and leadership skills. It is a good way to improve your career prospects, because volunteering looks great on a personal statement and a CV. If you know what kind of career you plan to aim for, then you could choose a volunteering job that will help you to gain experience that might give you the edge at an interview. For example, if you want to go into teaching, volunteering to tutor young children would be good.

Choosing what to do

There are lots of opportunities for volunteering, so how do you find the right one for you? To find a volunteer role that you enjoy and are capable of doing you should ask yourself the following questions:

- What kind of charities would you like to help?
- How much time can you give?
- Do you want to try something new or do something you know you're good at?
- Would you prefer to do something that is linked to the type of job you want in future?
- Would you like to do something with friends or linked to your class or school?

Your answers should help you pin down the type of charity you would like to help and the kind of volunteering you would like to do.

How to get involved

Many people start volunteering through their school, youth group, or college. We all have something different to offer, so think about what skills you have.

If you are good with young children, you could help out at your local leisure centre during the summer holidays as a play-scheme supervisor. If you are green-fingered you could help to plant flowers to beautify a park or children's play area in a deprived part of town. If you are good at organizing or persuading people to donate goods, you could collect tins of food or other necessities for emergency relief. If you are a computer whizz, you could use your skills to spread the word about a charity's work online.

Find out more about volunteering

You can search online for email addresses and contact telephone numbers of local, national, and international charities (see page 63 for some charity website links). You can find out more about volunteering at Volunteering England, Volunteering Wales, and Volunteering Scotland – charity and membership organizations that help and enable volunteers.

Get knitting!

Students from schools all over Australia got together during their lunch breaks to knit squares that were sewn into blankets for Save the Children Australia's "Knit One Save One" campaign. Thanks to the students' volunteering their time and effort, the charity was able to keep warm thousands of young children in India, Cambodia, Laos, and Australia.

Fundraising activities

Many young people become involved in fundraising efforts for a campaign they feel strongly about or a charity that their school or college supports. Raising funds can be fun and challenging, too. For example, planning a charity event can help you to develop both budgeting and planning skills. Schools and colleges are great places to raise money because you have access to a large number of people who are likely to support you.

You can select from a range of projects, from a sponsored litter clean-up on a beach, to a fashion show, disco, party, non-uniform day, or cake sale. You could try selling your artwork, holding a talent show, challenging parents or teachers to a sports match, or even a sponsored silence. If you contact the charity you are supporting before your event, they will often send you advice packs, publicity material, leaflets, banners, and balloons.

Serving others

"Imagine having a machine that can convert your winter-break boredom into fun, productive awesomeness. The Youth Volunteer Corps does just that. Our projects develop leadership skills, art skills, music skills ... computer hacking skills. I can imagine nothing more productive to do with your time than to become a youth volunteer. I wouldn't trade these times in for the world."

Ryan V., Youth Volunteer for the Youth Volunteer Corps in Southern Arizona, USA

Volunteering abroad

Volunteering abroad is a rich learning experience and a great way for teenagers to help others, travel, and learn about other cultures. Cross-Cultural Solutions (CCS) is a US-based charity that helps teenagers volunteer for community schemes in countries such as China, Costa Rica, and South Africa. Seventeen-year-old Melissa describes her experience:

> I worked at a school for persons with disabilities. Fellow CCS volunteers and I spackled [plastered] cinderblock walls of the school's new music room. We were preparing the walls so [that] fun, colourful murals could be painted on them. In addition, I played with the children on their playground, and even played soccer with some of the adults as well. Being around such individuals as those who attended the school gave me a new perspective on my own situation in life, and gave me an opportunity to spend time with these kids who seem to love life unconditionally.

> I had never spent that much time with a group of mentally disabled children, let alone those that do not speak English. I was worried that my basic (middle and high school) Spanish skills would prevent me from truly communicating with the students. However, I also saw this placement as a great opportunity. I feel that since I was able to comfortably interact with mentally disabled children and adults, in spite of a language barrier and behavioural differences, I can truly say that I am able to see people for who they are beneath the surface. It is a testament to understanding, equality, and compassion.

Face painting can be a good way to raise funds for charities.

1833 UK Factory Act bans children under nine from work and improves conditions for children working in factories

1853 Children's Aid Society is founded in the United States to take in street children

1867 Barnardo's starts helping the abused, vulnerable, and neglected children of London

1870 UK Education Act requires schools to be built for children aged 5 to 12

1870 By this year, all US states had free primary schools

1875 In the United, States, the New York Society for the Prevention of Cruelty to Children is formed, the first charity to protect abused children

1889 The National Society for the Prevention of Cruelty to Children (NSPCC) is formed in the United Kingdom

1889 The first Prevention of Cruelty to Children Act is passed in the United Kingdom

1904 The National Child Labor Committee is formed to eliminate child labour in the United States

1908 In the United Kingdom, the Children's Act establishes juvenile courts and introduces foster parent registration

1912 The Children's Bureau is founded in the United States to investigate child welfare

1919 Save the Children is founded in the United Kingdom to supply food to starving children in Austria after World War I

1919 The International Labour Organization starts to work against child labour

1923 Eglantyne Jebb (founder of Save the Children) writes the Declaration of the Rights of the Child

1924 The international organization, the League of Nations, adopts the Declaration of the Rights of the Child

1932 The UK Children and Young Persons Act broadens the powers of juvenile courts and introduces supervision orders for children at risk

1938 Fair Labor Standards Act outlaws child labour in the United States

1944 UK Education Act provides free primary and secondary education for all children and raises the school leaving age to 15

1946 UNICEF is created by the United Nations to provide aid to children after World War II

1948 UK Children Act establishes a children's committee and a children's officer in each local authority

1959 UN Declaration of the Rights of the Child defines children's rights to protection, education, health care, shelter, and good nutrition

1973 US Children's Defense Fund charity is formed to advocate for children's rights

1974 US Child Abuse Prevention and Treatment Act

1983 The Child Rights Information Network (CRIN) is founded to spread information about children's rights to NGOs and other groups

1988 The Global Polio Eradication Initiative begins to vaccinate children globally

1989 The UN Convention on the Rights of the Child expands children's rights and becomes the most widely accepted human rights treaty in history

1990 The UN World Summit for Children sets 10-year goals for children's health, nutrition, and education

1992 The formation of the International Programme for the Elimination of Child Labour within the International Labour Organization

2000 UN Millennium Development Goals include a decrease in child deaths worldwide by 2015

2001 The Measles Initiative is launched to reduce childhood deaths from measles worldwide

2002 UN treaty bans children under 18 from being recruited for armed combat

2010 Law in India makes education a fundamental right for children

GLOSSARY

abuse violent, harmful, cruel, or unfair treatment of a person or animal

addiction when someone is unable to stop taking harmful substances, such as drugs

agency organization or business that provides a particular service to another, such as aid to a government

AIDS see HIV/AIDS

alternative health therapist person who helps a patient using non-medical treatments such as acupuncture or herbs

campaign planned activities intended to achieve a particular aim, such as a set of newspaper adverts highlighting child abuse

child trafficking luring or kidnapping children to make them work for little or no money elsewhere

counsellor person trained to advise people about their personal problems

drop-in centre supervised place where people in need can go at any time for help, advice, or comfort

drought long period of time when there is very little or no rain

European Commission branch of the European Union that has some legal powers

European Union economic and political organization many European countries belong to

HIV/AIDS HIV is a virus that can cause AIDS, an illness that reduces the body's ability to resist infection and which usually results in death if not controlled

humanitarian working to help other people

hygiene practice of keeping clean to prevent illness and disease

latrine communal toilet block

less economically developed country (LEDC) one of the poorer countries of the world, including those in Africa, Asia (except for Japan), Latin America, and the Caribbean

malnutrition a condition that results from a poor diet that does not provide enough nutrients

media newspapers, magazines, radio, TV, the internet, and other forms of communication

mentor person with experience in a particular area who advises and helps someone with less experience. Mentor is also the name for that person.

more economically developed country (MEDC) one of the richer countries of the world, including those in Europe, North America, and Australia

non-governmental organization (NGO) a charity or association that is independent of government or business

outreach worker person who travels to provide a service or advice to people in need in their homes or communities

paediatrician doctor specializing in the treatment of children

petition written document signed by a large number of people that asks a person, organization, or government to do or change something

piecework work that is paid for by the amount done, not by the hours worked

polluted made unsafe or dirty by adding substances such as chemicals or waste to it

prosthetic plastic or metal body part that replaces a limb lost through accident or injury

psychologist person trained to understand how people think, act, react, and interact, and treat people to improve their mental health

refugee person who had to flee his or her country because of war or persecution (bad treatment)

right moral or legal claim to have or receive something or behave in a particular way. For example, according to international law, children have the right to an education and a safe home.

sanctioned legally forced to change his or her behaviour

sanitation equipment and systems to keep people clean, such as sewage pipes to remove human waste

slum area of city with extremely poor housing and a lack of basic services, such as running water and electricity

social worker person trained to investigate and help people who are disadvantaged in society

solar panel device that uses sunlight to produce electricity

sticky thread entry that will stay at the top of an online discussion site even if a new entry is posted

substance abuse using substances that are harmful, such as sniffing glue or injecting drugs

UNICEF an agency of the United Nations established in 1946 to help governments improve the health and education of children and their mothers

vaccination medicine usually given by injection to prevent someone catching a disease

volunteer person who works without being paid

web designer person who decides how websites should look and operate

FIND OUT MORE

Books

Celebrities Giving Back (How to Help: A Guide to Giving Back), Kayleen
  Reusser (Mitchell Lane Publishers, 2010)

UNICEF (Global Organizations), Sean Connolly (Franklin Watts, 2010)

Ways to Help Children with Disabilities (How to Help: A Guide to Giving Back),
  Karen Bush Gibson (Mitchell Lane Publishers, 2010)

Ways to Help Disadvantaged Youth (How to Help: A Guide to Giving Back),
  Laya Saul (Mitchell Lane Publishers, 2010)

We Are All Born Free: The Universal Declaration of Human Rights in Pictures,
  Amnesty International (Frances Lincoln Children's Books, 2008)

DVD

Children of War, directed by Bryan Single, rating 12A (see childrenofwarfilm.
com) about a group of Ugandan child soldiers, filmed inside a war zone.

Music

Listen to child soldier turned rapper Emmanuel Jal
www.npr.org/templates/story/story.php?storyId=4950821

Websites

UN website containing UNICEF's statistics about children's health, nutrition,
  and education: **www.childinfo.org/index.html**

UN website explaining the UN Convention of the Rights of the Child:
  www.unicef.org/rightsite/files/uncrcchilldfriendlylanguage.pdf

Charity website about street children: **streetaction.org/street-children**

A guide to child labour worldwide: **uk.oneworld.net/guides/childlabour**

UNHCR site about child refugees: **www.unhcr.org/pages/49c3646c1e8.html**

How water and sanitation affect children's health:
  www.who.int/ceh/risks/cehwater/en

A website about child soldiers: **www.child-soldier.org**

Other topics to research

You could also research how charities protect children facing other difficulties, such as children with disabilities, children who are carers for disabled or chronically ill adults or younger siblings, children who are in trouble with the law, or children who spend a lot of time in hospital.

Find out more about children's organizations in the book

Save the Children: **www.savethechildren.net/alliance/index.html**
UNICEF: **www.unicef.org**
Barnardo's: **www.barnardos.org.uk**
Blue Dragon Children's Foundation: **www.streetkidsinvietnam.com**
Help the Afghan Children: **www.helptheafghanchildren.org**
CARE: **www.care.org**
Play Pumps: **www.playpumps.co.za**
Computers for African Schools: **www.cfas.org.uk**
Rotary Youth Leadership Programmes: **www.rotary.org**
Big Brothers Big Sisters of America: **www.bbbs.org**
American Peace Corps: **www.peacecorps.gov**
1000 Days: **www.thousanddays.org**
Turning Wheels For Kids: **www.turningwheelsforkids.org**
Children in Need Institute: **www.cini-india.org**
Médecins Sans Frontières (Doctors Without Borders): **www.msf.org**
Sunshine Foundation of Canada: **www.sunshine.ca**
SunnyKids: **www.sunnykids.org.au**
Kids Company: **www.kidsco.org.uk**
International Initiative to End Child Labor: **www.endchildlabor.org**
Anti-Slavery International: **www.antislavery.org**
Oxfam: **www.oxfam.org**
War Child: **www.warchild.org**

If you have been affected by any of the issues in this book and you want to find out more or talk about it, contact the following helplines.

Childline UK calls are free and confidential, and you can chat to a counsellor online. Call 0800 1111 or see www.childline.org.uk/Talk/Pages/ContactingChildLine.aspx

The Runaway Helpline is a national 24-hour freephone helpline for anyone aged 17 or under who has run away or been forced to leave. Call 0808 800 70 70 or text 80234.

INDEX

LRC Radbrook